W9-ACC-871

JAMES A. GARFIELD

OUR TWENTIETH PRESIDENT

by Carol Brunelli

THE CHILD'S WORLD®

Published in the United States of America

The Child's World®
1980 Lookout Drive • Mankato, MN 56003-1705
800-599-READ • www.childsworld.com

Acknowledgments
The Child's World®: Mary Berendes, Publishing Director

Creative Spark: Mary McGavic, Project Director; Melissa McDaniel, Editorial
Director; Deborah Goodsite, Photo Research

The Design Lab: Kathleen Petelinsek, Design; Gregory Lindholm, Page Production

Content Adviser: David R. Smith, Adjunct Assistant Professor of History,
University of Michigan–Ann Arbor

Photos
Cover and page 3: White House Historical Association (White House Collection)
(detail); White House Historical Association (White House Collection)

Interior: Alamy: 7, 14 and 38 (North Wind Picture Archives); The Art Archive: 12
(Culver Pictures); The Bridgeman Art Library: 6 (Private Collection/Ken Welsh);
Corbis: 27, 33 (Corbis), 32, 36 and 39 (Bettmann); Getty Images: 21 and 39; The
Granger Collection, New York: 5, 17, 18, 20, 22, 29; iStockphoto: 44 (Tim Fan);
Lake County Historical Society, Painesville Township, Ohio: 4, 9, 11; Library of
Congress: 10 and 38, 15, 16, 23, 25, 26, 31, 37; North Wind Picture Archives: 8,
30, 34; Picture History: 19, 28; U.S. Air Force photo: 45; White House Historical
Association (White House Collection): 35.

Library of Congress Cataloging-in-Publication Data
Brunelli, Carol.
  James A. Garfield / by Carol Brunelli.
     p. cm. — (Presidents of the U.S.A.)
  Includes bibliographical references and index.
  ISBN 978–1–60253–049–2 (library bound : alk. paper)
  1. Garfield, James A. (James Abram), 1831–1881—Juvenile literature. 2.
Presidents—United States—Biography—Juvenile literature. I. Title. II. Series.

  E687.B878 2008
  973.8'4—dc22
  [B]
                              2008004370

Calvin Curtis painted this portrait of James Garfield in 1881.

TABLE OF CONTENTS

CHAPTER ONE

TEACHER AND PREACHER

On November 19, 1831, James Abram Garfield was born in northeastern Ohio in a log cabin built by his father. He was the youngest of Abram and Eliza Garfield's children. Just two years later, his father caught pneumonia and died, leaving James's mother to raise four young children alone. Eliza was a strong woman and very religious, and she worked hard to keep the farm and the family together. She taught her children important lessons about life.

Eliza Garfield was independent and determined.

The Garfield family farm had cows, hogs, and chickens. The family also raised corn and wheat, which they ate. But the first winter after the death of Abram was difficult for them. They had few crops to exchange for shoes, clothing, and food for the family. Sometimes there wasn't enough to eat, and Eliza Garfield would go to bed hungry, feeding her

growing boys and girls before herself. Soon she had to sell 50 acres to pay off a **debt.** To earn extra money, she took in sewing, spinning, and washing. Her eldest son, Thomas, worked on a neighbor's farm up to 14 hours a day. With the first handful of silver dollars he earned, Thomas bought little James—or Jimmy—Garfield his first pair of shoes.

James grew up with very little money, but he knew how to work hard for a better life. As a child, his poverty sometimes embarrassed him, but he later gained respect for what he accomplished in spite of it. His mother's faith helped him realize that he could achieve great things with his life even though he grew up poor.

James Garfield lived in the Ohio wilderness in a log cabin like this one.

The Garfield family had deep roots in the United States. Some of Garfield's **ancestors** arrived in Watertown, Massachusetts, in 1636.

Garfield was the last president to be born in a log cabin.

At age 16, James left home in search of adventure. He had always dreamed of becoming a sailor, so he went to the Cleveland waterfront. There he found a job as a canal boy. His main duty was to lead the horses that pulled barges along the Ohio and Pennsylvania Canal, a waterway used to transport goods and people. Strangely enough, James couldn't swim! He fell into the canal 14 times, but he was always saved by one of the lines that pulled the horses along. After six months of near misses, James decided that the life of a sailor wasn't for him and headed home. On the way, he came down with a serious fever. It lasted for nearly five months.

James Garfield was a bright child, learning to read at age three. This illustration from an early book about Garfield's life depicts him reading in the family's log cabin.

By March 1849, James was healthy again. He decided to reach for another dream. As a young boy, he had learned to read and write at a schoolhouse near his home, but he wanted more education. James enrolled at a school called the Geauga Academy. His family still had little money, so he worked his way through school by doing farm chores. He also taught some of the courses after he had completed them.

At his new school, James learned to love **debating.** This interest would last throughout his life. It helped him become an excellent public speaker after he entered **politics.** In his studies, James always did careful research on topics that interested him. This habit of careful study also helped him succeed.

Garfield worked for a time as a canal boy, leading horses that pulled barges along the water. Here, horses tow a barge along a canal in New York.

Garfield attended Williams College in northwestern Massachusetts. It is one of the country's leading colleges.

By the fall of 1851, James was ready for college. He entered Western Reserve Eclectic Institute (now called Hiram College). At college, he discovered that people liked to listen to him speak. He started preaching when he joined a church called the Disciples of Christ. James preached nearly every Sunday while he taught at the Eclectic Institute. Hundreds of people came to hear him. He continued to preach at church until he became a congressman.

In 1854, Garfield was prepared to continue his education at a **prestigious** eastern college. His top three choices were Yale, Brown, and Williams. He chose Williams College in Williamstown, Massachusetts.

Garfield was nearly 23 years old when he arrived at Williams, one of the oldest students on campus. He stood out in other ways, too. He was six feet tall and muscular, with blue eyes and thick, blond hair. He looked like a backwoodsman—a man living in the woods—in his rough western clothes. His eastern classmates stared at him, but he soon won their affection by his friendliness.

At Williams, Garfield studied **diligently,** determined to earn good grades. He joined debating groups, arguing about the issues of the day, and at the end of his first year was elected president of his class. One classmate described him as "undoubtedly one of the greatest debaters ever seen at Williams . . . [he] won and held the attention of this audience from the moment he opened his lips."

While Garfield was a student at the Western Reserve Eclectic Institute, he worked as a janitor to pay for his expenses. He built fires, swept floors, and rang the college bell.

During a winter break from Williams College, Garfield taught school in North Pownal, Vermont. Chester Arthur, the man who would one day be his vice president, had taught at the same school.

Garfield graduated from Williams College in 1856.

After two years at Williams, Garfield graduated with honors and returned to teach ancient languages and literature at the Western Reserve Eclectic Institute. He soon became president of the school.

In 1858, Garfield married one of his former students, Lucretia Rudolph, whom he called "Crete." He began to realize that he did not want to spend the rest of his life as a teacher. "My heart will never be satisfied to spend my life in teaching," he wrote to a friend. "I think there are other fields in which a man can do more."

About this time, Garfield became interested in politics. He also began to speak out against slavery, the most difficult problem the nation faced at the time. Slavery threatened the future of the nation. Many people in the northern states did not want slavery to expand into new states. Some wanted to end it entirely.

Garfield (at far left) taught a Greek class at the Western Reserve Eclectic Institute. He is shown here with his students, including Lucretia Rudolph, his future wife, who is seated beside him.

Like her husband, Lucretia Garfield was well-educated. She graduated from the Western Reserve Eclectic Institute and enjoyed translating Greek and Latin.

But people in the southern states were not willing to lose the free labor that enslaved workers provided. Southerners threatened to leave the United States if slavery was outlawed. They said they would create their own country. Like many people who opposed slavery, Garfield supported the Republican Party, one of the two major **political parties** of the day.

By 1859, Garfield had turned his love for preaching and teaching into a political career. He decided to run for the Ohio Senate. He was a good **candidate** because he was already well known to people in his hometown. Every time he gave a speech, Garfield spoke out against slavery. He was elected to the Ohio Senate less than two years before the Civil War would divide the nation.

Garfield sometimes entertained friends by writing in Latin with one hand and in Greek with the other.

11

JAMES GARFIELD'S RULES FOR LIVING

An elderly friend gave Garfield the following rules for living. Garfield tried to follow them until the end of his life.

- Never be idle.
- Make few promises.
- Always speak the truth.
- Live within your income.
- Never speak evil of anyone.
- Keep good company or none.
- Live up to your engagements.
- Never play games of chance.
- Drink no intoxicating [alcoholic] drinks.
- Good character is above everything else.
- Keep your own secrets if you have any.
- Never borrow if you can possibly help it.
- Do not marry until you are able to support a wife.
- When you speak to a person, look into his eyes.
- Save when you are young and spend when you are old.
- Never run into debt unless you can see a way out again.
- Good company and good conversation are the sinews of virtue.
- Your character cannot be essentially injured except by your own acts.
- If anybody speaks evil of you, let your life be so that no one believes him.
- When you retire at night think over what you have done during the day.
- If your hands cannot be employed usefully, attend to the culture of your mind.
- Read the above carefully and thoughtfully at least once a week.

SOLDIER AND CONGRESSMAN

In November 1860, Abraham Lincoln was elected president. Just one month later, the southern states started **seceding** from the **Union.** They refused to support a president whom they believed would work to end slavery. It seemed that the United States was about to split into two countries.

South Carolina was the first state to secede. Within seven months, a total of 11 southern states had left the Union and formed their own nation, which they called the Confederate States of America. In a letter to an old friend, Garfield wrote, "I do not see any way, outside a miracle of God, which can avoid civil war with all its attendant horrors."

Garfield was right. The country was soon at war. The Union did not have an army ready to fight. President Lincoln called on the states for 75,000 soldiers. Garfield was one of the men who **volunteered** to fight for the Union.

During the Civil War, Garfield quickly rose in rank. He entered the army as a lieutenant colonel. Just a few months later, he was promoted to the rank of colonel and put in charge of the 42nd Ohio Volunteer Regiment. His first battlefield assignment was to lead a brigade, a large group of soldiers. The brigade was sent to fight in Kentucky.

Garfield and his brigade were successful. They pushed the Confederates out of Kentucky. By 1862, Colonel Garfield was promoted to brigadier general. He left his regiment and led another brigade in battles at Shiloh and Corinth. Garfield wrote his wife about the Battle of Shiloh. "The horrible sights I have witnessed on this field, I can never describe," he said.

In November 1862, Garfield was elected to the House of Representatives, which is part of the U.S. Congress. He was still in the army at the time. Although

The Battle of Shiloh took place in southwestern Tennessee in April 1862. The fighting was brutal. Nearly 24,000 soldiers were wounded or killed.

Garfield (center) was a great soldier, and he quickly rose through the ranks of the Union army. By 1863, he was the youngest major general in the army.

Garfield was a dedicated soldier, he left the army to do his job as a congressman in Washington, D.C. President Lincoln helped Garfield make this decision. He told him that it was easier to find good generals than to find good Republicans for Congress. But before Garfield entered Congress, the army honored him once more by making him a major general.

Garfield took a short rest, returning to Ohio to be with his wife, their daughter, Eliza Arabella, and their infant son, Harry. Soon after Garfield's arrival, young Eliza died of **diphtheria.** She was just three years old. Not long after, Garfield left for the nation's capital city without his family. He felt sad and lonely as he entered the U.S. Congress in 1863. By the beginning of the

Garfield treasured time with his family. Here he is shown with his daughter, Mary.

In 1863, Congressman Garfield left Washington to see his wife. When he arrived home, she handed him a sheet of paper on which she had summed up the amount of time they had spent together. They had been married for nearly five years, but they had lived under the same roof for only 20 weeks. Garfield promised then and there that he would never again go to Washington without her.

next session, he had brought his family, including his mother, to Washington, where they would live throughout his career in politics. The family grew over the years, giving little Harry three happy, healthy, brothers named James, Abram, and Irvin, and a sister, Mary.

The Civil War ended in 1865. The South had lost, and enslaved people were freed. But the nation now had new problems to face. People worried about what would become of the former slaves. No one knew exactly how they would support themselves. No one knew how to protect them from southerners who still believed African Americans should be enslaved. The nation also faced the difficult job of reconstructing, or rebuilding, the South. The government had to decide how much power to give the states that had rebelled against the Union. This era in U.S. history is known as Reconstruction.

Garfield joined the Radical Republicans, a group of northern Republicans who wanted to punish the South. The Radical Republicans were determined that the ex-Confederates should suffer and struggle before they could rejoin the United States. Many Radical

When Garfield became a congressman in 1863, the dome of the Capitol was still under construction.

Republicans, including Garfield, supported **suffrage** for black men. Garfield voted for the Civil Rights Act of 1866, which gave people born into slavery U.S. citizenship. But he did not believe that this was enough to ensure their success. He believed education was the key to success for all Americans, black or white, northern or southern.

Garfield wanted equal educational opportunities for African Americans. He also supported the creation of a national Department of Education, which would oversee the creation of public schools. He favored educating deaf people and creating the museums of the Smithsonian Institution. Garfield also backed the creation of the U.S. Geological Survey. This government agency identifies land, water, energy, and mineral **resources.** It also creates maps and investigates hazards, such as earthquakes and volcanoes.

Before the Civil War, it was illegal to educate slaves. After the war, 3,000 schools were established to teach former slaves to read and write.

Garfield served in the U.S. House of Representatives from 1863 to 1880. During his many years in Congress, he became the most important Republican in the House. He was an expert on financial and educational issues. He served on many committees, such as the Committee on Banking and **Currency** and the Committee on the **Census.** He believed that collecting information about the American public with a census would allow the U.S. government to create better programs and services for its people. Many of Garfield's ideas were included in the 1880 census. Today the Census Bureau gathers information about the American people on many topics, such as health and education.

Garfield served in Congress for 17 years.

Garfield also believed that currency, or paper money, should be backed by gold. This means that the government would have gold **reserves** equal to the amount of currency that Americans were using. During the Civil War, the government printed more money than usual to help pay for the war. Dollars were worth less than before because there wasn't enough gold for each dollar. The Gold Act was finally passed in 1900, 19 years after Garfield died. But many people said that Garfield supported this act more than any other **politician** and helped it become a reality.

When Garfield entered Congress in 1863, he was the youngest member of the House of Representatives. He was 31 years old.

19

Chester A. Arthur was the Republican vice-presidential candidate in 1880.

Garfield was the only person in U.S. history to be a representative, senator-elect, and president-elect at the same time.

In January 1880, Garfield was elected to the U.S. Senate, but he never became a senator. Before his term began, the Republican Party chose him as their presidential candidate for the election of 1880. Chester A. Arthur was chosen as his running mate. Garfield told voters he was a self-made man—a man who had worked hard for everything he accomplished in his life, including his college education and his successful career in politics. During the **campaign,** Garfield gave speeches from his front porch. He was the first presidential candidate to do so. Unlike presidential candidates today, Garfield and many politicians after him stayed at home and the people came to them. Thousands of visitors traveled to Garfield's farm near Lake Erie. For months, news reporters camped on the lawn, ready to report on his latest speech.

When elections came in November, Garfield beat the Democratic candidate, General Winfield Scott Hancock, by only 10,000 popular votes (the votes of the American people). It was the closest popular election up to that time.

LIFE AFTER SLAVERY

After the Civil War ended, life was hard for African Americans
in the South. Most were illiterate, meaning they could not
read or write. When they tried to find jobs in factories, white
workers complained that the newly freed African Americans
were stealing their jobs. Many African Americans wanted
to own farms, but white landowners refused to sell them
land. Others would not rent land to former slaves or give
them bank loans. As a result, African Americans had no
choice but to work for white farmers. Usually, they barely
earned enough money to feed their families. James Garfield
wanted to improve this situation. He said, "We have seen
white men betray the flag and fight to kill the Union, but all
that long, dreary war, we never saw a traitor in black skin."

After the Civil War ended in 1865, Garfield voted for
black suffrage and supported equal educational opportunities
for blacks. When he became president in 1881, Garfield also
made sure to give government jobs to African Americans.

STALWARTS AND HALF-BREEDS

James A. Garfield became president in 1881. At 49 years old, he was the second-youngest United States president up to that time. He was a successful politician because he was hardworking and honest, which is what Americans wanted in their most important representative. He once said, "The people are responsible for the character of their Congress. If that body be ignorant, reckless, and **corrupt,** it is because the people tolerate ignorance, recklessness, and corruption. If it be intelligent, brave, and pure, it is because the people demand these high qualities to represent them." What Garfield meant is this: It is up to American voters to choose the best people for their government. If the nation's leaders are not honest or good, it is the fault of those who voted for them.

James A. Garfield in 1881

After the election, Garfield spent a few months at his Ohio farm, preparing for his life as the president of the United States. He knew that his private life would soon come to an end. He enjoyed quiet evenings by the fire with his wife and his private secretary, Joe Stanley-Brown, discussing the new problems that confronted him. In the mornings, he read piles of newspapers and letters coming in from all over the country. He rode about town on horseback tipping this hat to his friends and neighbors. But his peaceful country life did not last long.

Soon after Garfield was elected president, he found himself in the middle of a dangerous struggle for power. Two **factions** had formed within the Republican Party. They were called the Stalwarts and the Half-Breeds. These two groups were competing for positions in the new president's government. The Republicans had split into these factions more than four years earlier,

James Garfield was sworn in as president on March 4, 1881. That evening, a grand ball was held at the Arts and Industries Building, part of the Smithsonian Institution. It was the first event held in the building, which was not yet open to the public.

Garfield's 80-year-old mother, Eliza Garfield, was the first mother of a president to attend her son's **inauguration**.

Snow on the ground kept many people from attending Garfield's inauguration at the U.S. Capitol.

Garfield is one of only six left-handed presidents, and he was the first. The other five were: Truman, Ford, Reagan, the elder Bush, and Clinton.

when they could not agree on a presidential candidate during the election of 1876. The Stalwarts nicknamed their opponents "half-breeds," meaning that they were not true Republicans.

One task that President Garfield faced as soon as he entered office was to fill many government jobs. Prior to the start of his term, he had chosen his **cabinet,** which included the leaders of the departments of state, justice, treasury, war, navy, interior, and post office. Once he took office, hundreds of Republicans lined up outside the White House hoping to be chosen for one of the more than 100,000 government jobs available. Again and again, the White House staff had to turn away visitors. The line of people waiting to see the president stretched all the way to the street. "I received several thousand in the East Room," remembered Garfield.

Even with the help of his cabinet, interviewing all these people was an exhausting task. There were days when Garfield slept just a few hours. Whenever he had a free moment, Garfield tried to relax by spending time with his family, playing **billiards** and riding horseback along the Potomac River.

Problems between the Stalwarts and the Half-Breeds grew worse as soon as the president started filling high-ranking positions. Each faction wanted the president to choose its members. At first, the Stalwarts were pleased when the president recommended some of them for positions, even though Garfield himself was a Half-Breed. But a struggle developed when Garfield's

secretary of state, James Blaine, tried to replace several Stalwarts with Half-Breeds. Blaine wanted Half-Breed William H. Robertson to replace Stalwart Edwin A. Merritt as the collector of the port of New York. This position collected taxes on imports, which are goods brought into the United States from other countries. It was an important job because the port of New York handled more imports and collected more money than all other U.S. ports combined.

Senator Roscoe Conkling of New York, the leader of the Stalwarts, complained. The president tried to **compromise.** He promised Conkling that Merritt would remain the collector. But Garfield also told Conkling that Robertson would be appointed to a position as well. Conkling would not compromise— he did not want Robertson to have any position at all. The president grew tired of the tug-of-war between

In 1881, James and Lucretia Garfield and their five children, moved into the White House. Garfield's elderly mother lived in the White House with them.

This political cartoon shows President Garfield wrapping a ribbon tightly around Conkling (right) and Blaine. Garfield insisted on remaining independent in the battle between Stalwarts and Half-Breeds.

the factions, and he was angry about Conkling's stubbornness. Garfield made a decision: Robertson would get the position as collector. The Senate approved this choice, in part because the senators were pleased that Garfield had stood up to Conkling.

Garfield's showdown with Conkling impressed the public. It proved to Americans that no single person has the right to decide who will be an employee of the U.S. government—not an important person like Senator Conkling or even the president. Garfield made his choices for high-ranking government positions, but then the Senate decided whether to accept them.

GARFIELD STOPS A RIOT

On April 16, 1865, the day after Abraham Lincoln died, word began to spread about what had happened. The Civil War had just ended, and Americans were tense and afraid. With Lincoln's murder, the United States lost one of the greatest leaders in its history. Americans wondered what would happen next.

Garfield was in New York City that day. He came upon a crowd of about 50,000 people. Two men were lying in the street. They had been shot, and one of them was dead. Apparently, they had spoken against Lincoln, and someone in the angry mob that had formed shot them. The crowd was furious and seemed prepared for more violence. Garfield stepped into the crowd to calm them down. Soon he raised his right arm and began to preach. He sympathized with their fears. He assured them that their government was still strong and healthy. "Fellow citizens," he said, "God reigns and the government at Washington still lives." In the photograph below, a crowd in New York awaits President Lincoln's funeral procession.

CHAPTER FOUR

TRAGEDY IN WASHINGTON

By standing up to Conkling and the Stalwarts, Garfield showed both his opponents and the American people that he was a strong president. He proved that he would make his own decisions, even if members of his own political party disagreed with him.

Garfield wanted to do great things and set quickly to work. Soon after Garfield took office, he learned about a problem in the U.S. Postal Service. There were complaints that certain mail delivery routes, called Star Routes, were being run in a dishonest way. Star Routes delivered mail to areas of the South and the West that trains and steamships couldn't reach. The federal government

James Garfield was shot just four months after becoming president.

made agreements with horse, stagecoach, and wagon companies to deliver mail to these areas.

By 1880, there were 9,225 Star Routes, which cost almost $6 million to run. The cost was high because some companies tricked the U.S. government. They received the routes by charging a lower price than other companies, but once they had control of routes, they claimed that they had improved their service and needed more money. Sometimes they even charged for routes that did not exist.

In the 1800s, many Americans lived in remote areas that were hard to reach. The U.S. Postal Service relied on everything from horses to boats to deliver the mail. Here, a man wearing snowshoes delivers mail in the Rocky Mountains.

While Garfield was president, Clara Barton founded the American Red Cross.

Garfield's son James Rudolph was also a politician. He served in President Theodore Roosevelt's cabinet from 1907 to 1909.

This political cartoon shows one of Garfield's advisers, Thomas Brady, holding a bag of stars that symbolize the Star Routes of the Postal Service. When Garfield found out that Brady was involved in the scandal, he forced Brady to **resign.**

The government decided to investigate the Star Routes. It discovered that members of both the U.S. Postal Service and the Republican Party were involved in the corrupt actions. In fact, one of Garfield's advisers, Thomas Brady, was involved. Six weeks later, the president asked Brady to leave his position. Garfield would not stand for dishonesty among his aides.

As a congressman, Garfield had to deal with the nation's money matters. He continued to do this as president. He helped reduce the national debt, money that the country had borrowed and had to pay back. Garfield also wanted to improve the country's relations with Latin America. He asked Secretary of State Blaine to invite representatives from all nations in the

Americas to a conference. It was supposed to take place in Washington in 1882. The conference never took place. A terrible tragedy struck before it could be held.

After he became president, Garfield began to have nightmares about his own death. It was not the first time a president would have such terrible dreams. At a meeting, Garfield spoke with President Lincoln's son, Robert. Garfield asked him to describe the dreams his father had had just before he was **assassinated.** Lincoln explained that his father once dreamed of a dead body lying in the East Room of the White House. In the dream, Abraham heard someone crying. He asked a soldier standing guard, "Who is dead in the White

Mary, James, Harry, Irvin, and Abram Garfield were among the first young children of a president to live at the White House. Before Garfield, only Presidents Lincoln and Hayes had young families while they were in office.

Guiteau followed Garfield for several weeks before shooting him.

House?" The soldier replied, "The president." Hearing this story disturbed President Garfield.

After breakfast on the morning of July 2, 1881, Secretary of State Blaine and President Garfield went to the railroad station in Washington. They entered together walking side by side. There was a line of people waiting to buy tickets, but the depot wasn't too busy for a Saturday morning. Suddenly, while walking to the train, Garfield heard a loud, sharp sound like a firecracker and felt a sting in his right side. Then he heard another sound and felt a pain in his back. He spun around and fell to the ground. The president had been shot twice by a man named Charles J. Guiteau. Guiteau was standing just six feet behind him. After shooting the president, Guiteau walked calmly through the main hall of the railroad station toward the exit as though nothing had happened. He still had the pistol in his hand. Blaine turned to chase the shooter but then saw the president lying on the floor bleeding and ran back to his side.

Guiteau was an unstable man. He had been a preacher, lawyer, and debt collector, but he was always changing jobs and moving from one city to another. In 1880, he became interested in politics and in writing speeches for political candidates. Guiteau had supported Garfield during his election. He had even written a pamphlet to help him win. Guiteau hoped that Garfield would give him an important government position when he became president. He was one of the many job seekers that lined up at the White House soon after the election. His personal requests to the president and to cabinet members were rejected again and again. Finally, Secretary of State Blaine told him never to return. Guiteau became angry and decided to kill the president.

Guiteau was arrested on the spot and taken to nearby police headquarters. When asked why he had shot the president, he replied, "To save the Republican Party. . . . I am a Stalwart, among Stalwarts." The following year, Guiteau was tried and convicted of the murder and hanged.

The morning of the shooting, Garfield took a challenge from his son Harry to jump all the way over a bed—he did it!

In 1882, it took a jury just one hour to find Charles Guiteau guilty of murder.

James A. Garfield was the second president to be shot while in office. Abraham Lincoln was the first.

Garfield's wife stayed by his bedside for 80 days after he was shot.

President Garfield did not die right away. At first, he was treated in the White House. An expensive air-conditioning system was installed to keep him cool in the sweltering summer heat. It used 100 pounds of ice each hour. Week after week, Americans waited to hear news about the president's condition. Garfield himself tried to reassure the public, saying, "It is true I am still weak, and on my back; but I am gaining every day, and need only time and patience to bring me through."

Two months after he was shot, the president seemed to be doing better. He asked to be moved to New Jersey, hoping to recover by the seashore. A team of 300 men laid a half-mile railroad track so that a special train could take the president right to the front door of his cottage by the sea. Unfortunately, Garfield's condition grew worse after he arrived in New Jersey.

Workers lay a railroad track to Garfield's home in Elberon, New Jersey. The men laid the half-mile (1 km) of track in less than 24 hours.

On September 19, 1881, President James Abram Garfield died from infection and internal bleeding. His wife was by his side. The nation mourned, for Garfield had made the country better and stronger. He also left a good example for future presidents. He did not give in to powerful political parties. He did not accept dishonesty in the government.

In 1879, lawyer and novelist Albion W. Tourgée wrote a book called *Figs and Thistles.* Many believed this book was about the life of James Garfield. It was a story of a poor, fatherless boy who worked his way through school and grew up to be president of the United States. Tourgée's story had a happy ending. Unfortunately, Garfield's story did not. But this preacher, teacher, and leader gave the country hope for an honest government and a strong nation.

After President Garfield died, the White House was draped with black fabric to express the nation's grief.

SCIENCE AND THE DEATH
OF A PRESIDENT

James Garfield lived for more than two months after he was shot. Doctors tried many times to remove the bullet that was lodged in his body, but they couldn't find it. Two scientists, Simon Newcomb and Alexander Graham Bell, tried to help. Newcomb was experimenting with running electricity through wire coils. He found that when metal was placed near the coils, he could hear a faint hum. He hoped to perfect his invention so that it could be used to locate the bullet.

Bell read about Newcomb in a newspaper. He offered his help, suggesting that his invention, the telephone, might be able to improve Newcomb's invention. It could make the humming sound louder. The two men joined forces and came up with an early version of a metal detector.

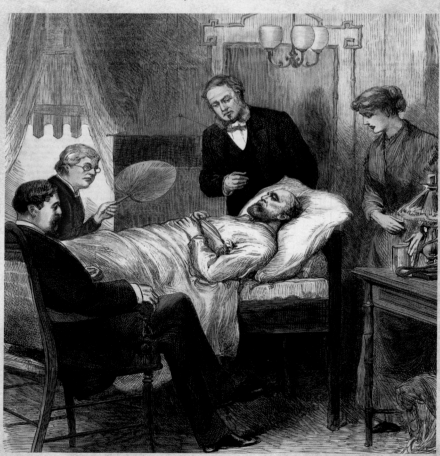

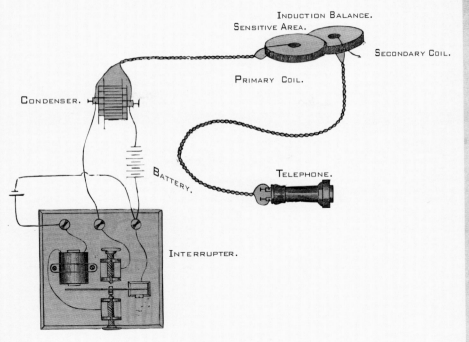

INDUCTION BALANCE.
SENSITIVE AREA.
SECONDARY COIL.
PRIMARY COIL.
CONDENSER.
BATTERY.
TELEPHONE.
INTERRUPTER.

PROF. A. GRAHAM BELL'S INDUCTION-BALANCE FOR ASCERTAINING
THE LOCATION OF A BULLET IN A HUMAN BODY.

On July 26, Bell and Newcomb went to the White House to try their invention. The detector made a humming sound no matter where they placed it on the president's body. Bell and Newcomb left the White House confused and disappointed. Why didn't their invention work?

Bell returned to the lab with Newcomb. They ran more experiments, and their invention worked well. They returned to the White House on the last day of July. The same thing happened. No matter where they placed the detector on the president's body, they heard a faint hum.

What was wrong with Bell and Newcomb's invention? The invention wasn't the problem. The problem was the president's bed! It had springs made of metal, so the metal detector kept humming and humming. The White House was one of the few places that had mattresses with metal springs at the time. If Bell and Newcomb had moved the president off the bed and onto the floor, their invention could have found the bullet.

It is still likely that Garfield would have died, however. Doctors had probed for the bullet with their dirty hands and instruments. This had brought germs into Garfield's wounds, causing severe infection.

1830   **1840**   **1850**

1831
James A. Garfield is born on November 19 in northern Ohio.

1833
Garfield's father dies, leaving Garfield's mother, Eliza, to raise the children and run the family farm.

1848
Garfield leaves home to become a canal boy on the Cleveland waterfront.

1849
Garfield begins taking classes at Geauga Academy. He teaches and takes carpentry jobs to pay for school.

1851
Garfield enters Western Reserve Eclectic Institute (now Hiram College). He joins a church called the Disciples of Christ and begins preaching.

1854
Garfield enters Williams College in Massachusetts.

1856
Garfield graduates from Williams College and becomes a professor at the Western Reserve Eclectic Institute. He teaches ancient languages and literature.

1857
Garfield becomes the president of the Western Reserve Eclectic Institute. He holds the position until 1861, when the Civil War begins.

1858
Garfield marries Lucretia "Crete" Randolph.

1859
Garfield is elected to the Ohio State Senate.

1860
Abraham Lincoln is elected president. Southern states begin to secede from the Union.

1861
The Civil War begins. Garfield volunteers as a soldier for the Union army.

1862
Garfield is promoted to the rank of brigadier general. In November, he is elected to the House of Representatives. Soon after, he is promoted to major general. He resigns from the army to take his seat in the House.

1865
On April 9, Confederate general Robert E. Lee surrenders, ending the Civil War. On April 14, President Lincoln is assassinated. The Reconstruction era begins. Garfield joins forces with the Radical Republicans, who believe southerners must be held responsible for the rebellion. He supports voting rights and education for African Americans.

1869
As a congressman, Garfield fights for the creation of a Census Bureau.

1877
Reconstruction ends.

1879
The U.S. Geological Survey is created, which Garfield has supported in the House of Representatives.

1880
Garfield is elected senator. He is then chosen to be the Republican presidential candidate. He runs a "front-porch campaign" from his home in Mentor, Ohio. He wins the election in November.

1881
Garfield is sworn in as the 20th president of the United States on March 4. In office, he struggles with problems between different factions in the Republican Party. He also fights dishonest activities in the U.S. Postal Service and encourages better relations with Latin America. On July 2, Charles J. Guiteau shoots Garfield. Guiteau is a former supporter of Garfield who is angry that he did not receive a government job. Doctors cannot find the bullet lodged in Garfield's body. The president dies 11 weeks after the shooting, on September 19, 1881. Guiteau is hanged for the murder.

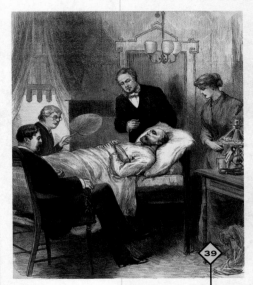

39

GLOSSARY

ancestors (AN-sess-turz) Ancestors are relatives who were born a long time ago. Garfield had ancestors that came to Massachusetts in 1636.

assassinated (uh-SASS-ih-nayt-ed) If someone is assassinated, that means he or she was murdered. President Garfield was the second president to be assassinated.

billiards (BIL-yurdz) Billiards is a game played on a cloth-covered table with pockets, similar to pool. Playing billiards was one of Garfield's favorite ways of relaxing.

cabinet (KAB-nit) A cabinet is the group of people who advise a president. Garfield's son served in President Theodore Roosevelt's cabinet.

campaign (kam-PAYN) A campaign is the process of running for an election, including activities such as giving speeches or attending rallies. Garfield ran a "front-porch campaign" from his home.

candidate (KAN-duh-dayt) A candidate is a person running in an election. Garfield was the Republican Party's presidential candidate in 1880.

census (SEN-sus) A census is an official count of the people in a country or district. It is taken to find out the number of people in the area, their ages, what they do for a living, and other facts.

compromise (KOM-pruh-myz) A compromise is a way to settle a disagreement in which both sides give up part of what they want. Garfield tried to reach a compromise with Senator Conkling over government jobs.

corrupt (ku-RUPT) If people are corrupt, they act improperly for their own benefit, such as by taking bribes. Some officials in the U.S. Postal Service were corrupt.

currency (KUR-unt-see) Currency is paper money. Garfield believed that U.S. currency should be backed by gold reserves.

debating (di-BAY-ting) Debating means taking part in a contest in which opponents argue for opposite sides of an issue. Garfield enjoyed debating.

debt (DET) Debt is money that is owed. Garfield helped reduce the national debt.

diligently (DIL-uh-jent-lee) To do something diligently is to give all of one's effort and attention to it. Garfield worked diligently to achieve his goals.

diphtheria (dip-THEER-ee-uh) Diphtheria is a disease that causes the heart to swell. Garfield's daughter died from diphtheria.

factions (FAK-shenz) Factions are small groups within a bigger organization, such as a political party. The Stalwarts and the Half-Breeds were factions in the Republican Party.

inauguration (ih-nawg-yuh-RAY-shun)
An inauguration is the ceremony that takes place when a new president begins a term. Garfield's mother attended his inauguration.

political parties (puh-LIT-ih-kul PAR-teez)
Political parties are groups of people who share similar ideas about how to run a government. Garfield supported the Republican political party.

politician (pawl-ih-TISH-un) A politician is a person who holds an office in government. James Garfield had been a politician for many years when he was elected president.

politics (PAWL-uh-tiks) Politics refers to the actions and practices of the government. Garfield became interested in politics while he was an educator.

prestigious (preh-STI-jus) Prestigious means having a good reputation or great influence. Garfield attended Williams, a prestigious college.

reserves (reh-ZURVZ) Reserves are valuable assets, such as money or gold, that are saved for a special reason. At one time, the U.S. government had gold reserves that equaled the amount of dollars in circulation.

resign (ri-ZYNE) If someone resigns, he or she quits a job. Garfield resigned from the army after he was elected to the U.S. House of Representatives.

resources (REE-sor-sez) Resources are supplies of useful things, such as minerals, water, or land. The U.S. Geological Survey studies the nation's natural resources.

seceding (suh-SEED-ing) If a group is seceding, it is separating from a larger group. Eleven southern states seceded from the Union between 1860 and 1861.

secretary of state (SEK-ruh-tayr-ee OF STAYT) The secretary of state is a close adviser to the president. He or she is involved with the country's relations with other nations.

suffrage (SUH-frij) Suffrage is the right to vote. Garfield supported suffrage for African American men.

Union (YOON-yen) The Union is another name for the United States of America. During the Civil War, the North was called the Union.

volunteered (vol-un-TEERD) If someone volunteered, he or she offered to do a job. Garfield volunteered for the Union army.

THE UNITED STATES GOVERNMENT

T he United States government is divided into three equal branches: the executive, the legislative, and the judicial. This division helps prevent abuses of power because each branch has to answer to the other two. No one branch can become too powerful.

EXECUTIVE BRANCH

PRESIDENT
VICE PRESIDENT
DEPARTMENTS

The job of the executive branch is to enforce the laws. It is headed by the president, who serves as the spokesperson for the United States around the world. The president signs bills into law and appoints important officials such as federal judges. He or she is also the commander in chief of the U.S. military. The president is assisted by the vice president, who takes over if the president dies or cannot carry out the duties of the office.

The executive branch also includes various departments, each focused on a specific topic. They include the Defense Department, the Justice Department, and the Agriculture Department. The department heads, along with other officials such as the vice president, serve as the president's closest advisers, called the cabinet.

LEGISLATIVE BRANCH

CONGRESS
Senate and
House of Representatives

The job of the legislative branch is to make the laws. It consists of Congress, which is divided into two parts: the Senate and the House of Representatives. The Senate has 100 members, and the House of Representatives has 435 members. Each state has two senators. The number of representatives a state has varies depending on the state's population.

Besides making laws, Congress also passes budgets and enacts taxes. In addition, it is responsible for declaring war, maintaining the military, and regulating trade with other countries.

JUDICIAL BRANCH

SUPREME COURT
COURTS OF APPEALS
DISTRICT COURTS

The job of the judicial branch is to interpret the laws. It consists of the nation's federal courts. Trials are held in district courts. During trials, judges must decide what laws mean and how they apply. Courts of appeals review the decisions made in district courts.

The nation's highest court is the Supreme Court. If someone disagrees with a court of appeals ruling, he or she can ask the Supreme Court to review it. The Supreme Court may refuse. The Supreme Court makes sure that decisions and laws do not violate the Constitution.

CHOOSING
THE PRESIDENT

It may seem odd, but American voters don't elect the president directly. Instead, the president is chosen using what is called the Electoral College.

Each state gets as many votes in the Electoral College as its combined total of senators and representatives in Congress. For example, Iowa has two senators and five representatives, so it gets seven electoral votes. Although the District of Columbia does not have any voting members in Congress, it gets three electoral votes. Usually, the candidate who wins the most votes in any given state receives all of that state's electoral votes.

To become president, a candidate must get more than half of the Electoral College votes. There are a total of 538 votes in the Electoral College, so a candidate needs 270 votes to win. If nobody receives 270 Electoral College votes, the House of Representatives chooses the president.

With the Electoral College system, the person who receives the most votes nationwide does not always receive the most electoral votes. This happened most recently in 2000, when Al Gore received half a million more national votes than George W. Bush. Bush became president because he had more Electoral College votes.

THE WHITE HOUSE

The White House is the official home of the president of the United States. It is located at 1600 Pennsylvania Avenue NW in Washington, D.C. In 1792, a contest was held to select the architect who would design the president's home. James Hoban won. Construction took eight years.

The first president, George Washington, never lived in the White House. The second president, John Adams, moved into the house in 1800, though the inside was not yet complete. During the War of 1812, British soldiers burned down much of the White House. It was rebuilt several years later.

The White House was changed through the years. Porches were added, and President Theodore Roosevelt added the West Wing. President William Taft changed the shape of the presidential office, making it into the famous Oval Office. While Harry Truman was president, the old house was discovered to be structurally weak. All the walls were reinforced with steel, and the rooms were rebuilt.

Today, the White House has 132 rooms (including 35 bathrooms), 28 fireplaces, and 3 elevators. It takes 570 gallons of paint to cover the outside of the six-story building. The White House provides the president with many ways to relax. It includes a putting green, a jogging track, a swimming pool, a tennis court, and beautifully landscaped gardens. The White House also has a movie theater, a billiard room, and a one-lane bowling alley.

PRESIDENTIAL PERKS

The job of president of the United States is challenging. It is probably one of the most stressful jobs in the world. Because of this, presidents are paid well, though not nearly as well as the leaders of large corporations. In 2007, the president earned $400,000 a year. Presidents also receive extra benefits that make the demanding job a little more appealing.

★ **Camp David:** In the 1940s, President Franklin D. Roosevelt chose this heavily wooded spot in the mountains of Maryland to be the presidential retreat, where presidents can relax. Even though it is a retreat, world business is conducted there. Most famously, President Jimmy Carter met with Middle Eastern leaders at Camp David in 1978. The result was a peace agreement between Israel and Egypt.

★ *Air Force One*: The president flies on a jet called *Air Force One*. It is a Boeing 747-200B that has been modified to meet the president's needs.

Air Force One is the size of a large home. It is equipped with a dining room, sleeping quarters, a conference room, and office space. It also has two kitchens that can provide food for up to 50 people.

★ **The Secret Service:** While not the most glamorous of the president's perks, the Secret Service is one of the most important. The Secret Service is a group of highly trained agents who protect the president and the president's family.

★ **The Presidential State Car:** The presidential limousine is a stretch Cadillac DTS.

It has been armored to protect the president in case of attack. Inside the plush car are a foldaway desk, an entertainment center, and a communications console.

★ **The Food:** The White House has five chefs who will make any food the president wants. The White House also has an extensive wine collection.

★ **Retirement:** A former president receives a pension, or retirement pay, of just under $180,000 a year. Former presidents also receive Secret Service protection for the rest of their lives.

FACTS

QUALIFICATIONS

To run for president, a candidate must

- ★ be at least 35 years old
- ★ be a citizen who was born in the United States
- ★ have lived in the United States for 14 years

TERM OF OFFICE

A president's term of office is four years.
No president can stay in office for more than two terms.

ELECTION DATE

The presidential election takes place every four years on the first Tuesday of November.

INAUGURATION DATE

Presidents are inaugurated on January 20.

OATH OF OFFICE

I do solemnly swear I will faithfully execute the office of the President of the United States and will to the best of my ability preserve, protect, and defend the Constitution of the United States.

WRITE A LETTER TO THE PRESIDENT

One of the best things about being a U.S. citizen is that Americans get to participate in their government. They can speak out if they feel government leaders aren't doing their jobs. They can also praise leaders who are going the extra mile. Do you have something you'd like the president to do? Should the president worry more about the environment and encourage people to recycle? Should the government spend more money on our schools? You can write a letter to the president to say how you feel!

1600 Pennsylvania Avenue
Washington, D.C. 20500
You can even send an e-mail to: president@whitehouse.gov

BOOKS

Ackerman, Kenneth. *Dark Horse: The Surprise Election and Political Murder of President James A. Garfield.* New York: Carroll & Graf Publishers, 2003.

Doak, Robin. *James A. Garfield.* Minneapolis: Compass Point Books, 2003.

Feldman, Ruth Tenzer. *James A. Garfield.* Breckenridge, CO: Twenty-First Century Books, 2005.

Greene, Meg. *Into the Land of Freedom: African Americans in Reconstruction.* Minneapolis: Lerner, 2004.

Heinrichs, Ann. *Lucretia Rudolph Garfield: 1832–1918.* Chicago: Children's Press, 1998.

Kent, Deborah. *James A. Garfield: America's 20th President.* New York: Children's Press, 2004.

McPherson, James. *Fields of Fury: The American Civil War.* New York: Atheneum Books for Young Readers, 2002.

VIDEOS

The History Channel Presents The Presidents. DVD (New York: A&E Home Video, 2005).

National Geographic's Inside the White House. DVD (Washington, DC: National Geographic Video, 2003).

INTERNET SITES

Visit our Web page for lots of links about James A. Garfield and other U.S. presidents:

http://www.childsworld.com/links

Note to Parents, Teachers, and Librarians: We routinely verify our Web links to make sure they are safe, active sites—so encourage your readers to check them out!

INDEX